THE GREAT DEPRESSION

History SparkNotes

SPARKNOTES is a registered trademark of SparkNotes LLC

Spark Publishing
A Division of Barnes & Noble Publishing
120 Fifth Avenue
New York, NY 10011
www.sparknotes.com

ISBN-13: 978-1-4114-0425-0
ISBN-10: 1-4114-0425-4

Library of Congress information available upon request.

Please submit changes or report errors to www.sparknotes.com/errors.

Printed and bound in the United States.

1 3 5 7 9 10 8 6 4 2

CONTENTS

OVERVIEW

B eginning in 1929, the United States saw one of the most dramatic upheavals in its history, in just a few short years the nation crashed precipitously from the prosperity and glamour of the Roaring Twenties to the desperate hardship and poverty of the Great Depression. Never had the highs been higher or the lows been lower. The Great Depression—the worst economic crisis in the country's history—left an indelible scar on American society and culture, causing millions of people to languish in joblessness, homelessness, and starvation for nearly a decade. In an American culture that measured self-worth by success, many breadwinners from the Roaring Twenties felt deep humiliation when they found themselves unable even to put food on their families' tables. Even today, nearly every survivor of the Great Depression can still recall the feelings of hunger and desperation.

The Great Depression in the United States also caused a major worldwide depression, as virtually every industrialized economy— Britain, France, Italy, Germany, Japan, and others—was brought to its knees in the 1930s. The fiscally conservative U.S. government, led by then-president Herbert Hoover, refused to provide any direct relief to the masses. Britain and France took out their economic woes on Germany and demanded payment of exorbitantly large World War I reparations. In this sense, Germany was perhaps hit the hardest, as its economy had already experienced the devastating effects of hyperinflation before the U.S. stock market crashed in 1929. The German economy was saved from complete collapse— only temporarily—by the United States' offer of the 1924 Dawes Plan to reschedule reparation payments. Even with the aid, the emerging German leader, Adolf Hitler, could only make vague promises to strengthen and revitalize the country's failing economy.

Not until the presidency of Franklin Delano Roosevelt did the United States begin its long, slow recovery process. FDR's New Deal policies and programs not only provided relief, recovery, and reform but also drastically changed the federal government's role in politics and society. During FDR's terms in office in the 1930s, the federal government had unprecedented control over and direct involvement in the daily lives of American people. Many critics denounced the New Deal, saying that the policies were transforming the United States into a welfare state. Indeed, the budget deficit skyrocketed every year and the national debt more than doubled in just ten years. Roosevelt applied the economic theories of John Maynard Keynes to his new domestic policies, and the positive results were so widespread that even long after the Great Depression was over, Democrats continued to fight for more government intervention in the economy, greater redistribution of wealth, and increased aid for the neediest.

Despite the criticism that the New Deal attracted, its policies and legislation must be considered a success simply by virtue of the fact that they enabled millions of Americans to survive the Great Depression. Unlike his Republican predecessor, Hoover, Roosevelt's goal was to help as many Americans as possible, regardless of Congress's or the Supreme Court's disapproval. Whereas Hoover's perspective had been to wait for the storm to pass and let the economy correct itself, Roosevelt took immediate action, passing legislation that created new jobs, constructed houses and shelters, and handed out food to the hungry. Roosevelt did not stop with the average American: he helped inflate agricultural commodity prices in order to assist farmers, he helped banks return to solid ground, and he greatly improved the national infrastructure through public works programs.

Despite these numerous benefits, however, the New Deal ultimately failed to end the Great Depression. More than ten years after the Crash of 1929, millions of Americans were still hungry, homeless, and unemployed. Some historians argue that Roosevelt could have ended the depression completely if he had put more federal dollars into the economy, but this conclusion is debatable. The depression ended only after the United States entered World War II in 1941, when the increased demand for wartime commodities such as ships, tanks, and munitions gave the U.S. economy the jump start it needed.

SUMMARY OF EVENTS

HARDING AND COOLIDGE

In 1920, President **Warren G. Harding**'s election heralded a new age of political and economic conservatism. The Republican Congress, for example, passed the **Esch-Cummins Transportation Act** in 1920 to deregulate the railroads and return them to private control. Also under Harding, Congress passed the 1922 **Fordney-McCumber Tariff**, which raised the average protective tariff rate to a new high of nearly 40 percent. Furthermore, the conservative Supreme Court reversed their previous *Adkins v. Children's Hospital* ruling, stripping women workers of all special labor protection. This reversal came just after the ratification of the **Nineteenth Amendment** in 1920, which granted women the right to vote.

As a result of the resurgence of political and economic conservatism, big business reigned supreme once again, and labor movements dwindled. Instances of government corruption, such as the **Teapot Dome scandal**, were relatively frequent during Harding's presidency, and in some cases the money trail led all the way to the president himself. When Harding died unexpectedly in 1923, the even more conservative **Calvin Coolidge** became president and continued to push his predecessor's conservative policy. Coolidge was then elected to another term in the three-way election of 1924.

ISOLATIONISM

Harding's and Coolidge's stances on foreign policy were a reflection of Americans' isolationist attitudes, and both presidents worked hard to reduce the United States' influence abroad. Harding, for example, negotiated the **Five-Power Naval Treaty** in 1922 to reduce the number of American, British, and Japanese battleships in the Pacific. The same year, France, Britain, Japan, and the United States signed the **Four-Power Treaty** to guarantee the territorial status quo in the Pacific region and joined other European and Asian powers in signing the **Nine-Power Treaty** to uphold the Open Door policy in China. Furthermore, Coolidge's secretary of state rather naively signed the 1928 **Kellogg-Briand Pact** (along with sixty other nations) to outlaw aggressive warfare. Coolidge's vice president also drew up the **Dawes Plan**, which arranged a new timetable for impoverished Germany to pay off its World War I reparations to Britain and France.

THE ROARING TWENTIES

The **Roaring Twenties** ushered in an exciting time of social change and economic prosperity, as the recession at the end of World War I was quickly replaced by an unprecedented period of financial growth. The stock market soared to unimaginable heights, buoyed by the so-called **second Industrial Revolution** of the turn of the twentieth century, which saw the development of new inventions and machines that changed American society drastically. For example, industry leader **Henry Ford** developed the **assembly line**, which enabled mass production of the **automobile**—the invention that changed the nation more than any other during the era. The car helped give rise to **suburban** America, as thousands of middle-class Americans left the congested cities for nicer communities in the city outskirts. The **airplane**, **radio**, and **motion picture** ranked with the automobile as popular new inventions of the time. At the same time, a new age of American literature blossomed in the 1920s.

THE RED SCARE AND IMMIGRATION RESTRICTIONS

This social revolution of the 1920s was not without its darker side. Sudden changes in the social fabric spawned a reactionary backlash in the name of preserving American heritage, tradition, and culture. The **Red Scare** of 1919–1920, in which hundreds of socialists were persecuted, was just the first instance. The more sweeping **Emergency Quota Act** and **Immigration Act of 1924** effectively slammed the door shut on all "undesirable" and "unassimilable" immigrants.

Anticommunist and anti-immigration sentiments notoriously culminated in the infamous **Sacco-Vanzetti Trial** of 1921. In the trial, two Italian-born Americans, both atheists and anarchists, were convicted of murder and executed even though there was no hard evidence that they had committed the crime.

PROHIBITION AND FUNDAMENTALISM

Around the same time, conservative "drys" scored a major victory when in 1919 the **Eighteenth Amendment** was ratified and the **Volstead Act** was passed. These new laws began fourteen years of **Prohibition**, in which the consumption, sale, and manufacture of alcohol were made illegal under U.S. law. Not until 1933, when the **Twenty-First Amendment** repealed Prohibition, was alcohol once again legal.

Also during this period, Christian fundamentalists rallied together against **Charles Darwin**'s theory of **natural selection**, which they saw as heresy. These fundamentalists lost a great deal of credi-

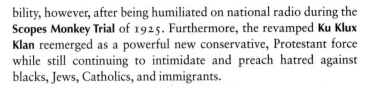

bility, however, after being humiliated on national radio during the **Scopes Monkey Trial** of 1925. Furthermore, the revamped **Ku Klux Klan** reemerged as a powerful new conservative, Protestant force while still continuing to intimidate and preach hatred against blacks, Jews, Catholics, and immigrants.

HOOVER AND THE CRASH OF 1929

Elected president in 1928, **Herbert Hoover**, a popular administrative hero of **World War I**, promised more prosperity and more boons for big business. Hoover tried to remain true to his word even after the stock market crashed on **Black Tuesday** in October 1929. He promised that the recession resulting from the **Crash of 1929** would be brief and that prosperity was just around the corner. Rather than offer a helping hand, however, Hoover and congressional Republicans passed the even higher **Smoot-Hawley Tariff** in 1930, driving the average tariff rate up to almost 60 percent.

THE DEPRESSION BEGINS

The American economy quickly slipped into recession and then plummeted headlong into the greatest depression the nation had ever experienced. The **Great Depression** in the United States had a widespread ripple effect throughout the world, soon leading to economic stagnation and widespread unemployment in virtually every industrialized nation. Millions of Americans lost their jobs and their homes, and shantytowns dubbed **"Hoovervilles"** (after the president whom many blamed for the depression) began to spring up throughout the country.

Despite the worsening economic plight, Hoover still refused to provide any direct federal assistance to relieve the suffering. He even authorized the army to use force to remove 20,000 members of the **"Bonus Army,"** a group of World War I veterans and their families who marched on the U.S. Capitol demanding economic relief. By 1932, Americans, fed up with Hoover's lack of economic assistance, voted him and his Republican counterparts out of office. The optimistic Democrat **Franklin Delano Roosevelt** of New York—a distant cousin of previous president Theodore Roosevelt—took office.

ROOSEVELT'S NEW DEAL: RELIEF, RECOVERY, AND REFORM

Roosevelt rallied the panicked Democratic majority in Congress and pushed for the passage of a bundle of sweeping laws known collectively as the **New Deal**. Taking a calculated risk, Roosevelt structured the New Deal policies around the untested theories of

British economist **John Maynard Keynes,** who believed that planned deficit spending by the federal government could "prime the economic pump" and jump-start the economy again.

THE FIRST HUNDRED DAYS

During Roosevelt's **First Hundred Days** in office, he and Congress passed the bulk of the legislation of the **First New Deal.** The first thing Roosevelt did was to declare a national **bank holiday** so that banks could reopen the following week on more stable footing. The **Emergency Banking Relief Act** also gave the president control over exchange rates and all banking transactions. Additionally, the **Glass-Steagall Banking Reform Act** created the **Federal Deposit Insurance Corporation (FDIC)** to insure individual deposits with government money. The FDIC helped restore the public's confidence in banks, as many people had lost their savings when banks failed after the stock market crash of 1929. The FDIC made sure that Americans would not lose their savings if a bank ever collapsed again.

THE "ALPHABET AGENCIES"

The New Deal created the **Agricultural Adjustment Administration (AAA)** to provide federal subsidies to farmers and created countless new jobs through the formation of the **Civil Conservation Corps (CCC),** the **Civil Works Administration (CWA),** the **Public Works Administration (PWA),** and the **Tennessee Valley Authority (TVA).** The **Federal Emergency Relief Administration (FERA)** was also established to provide relief on the state level, while the **National Industrial Recovery Act (NIRA)** was passed to bail out the nation's failing factories.

THE SECOND NEW DEAL

Criticism from both conservatives and liberals prompted Roosevelt to push a second wave of New Deal legislation through Congress from 1935 to 1936, in a collective package known as the **Second New Deal.** This legislation included the sweeping **Social Security Act** to provide government pensions to the elderly, the **Indian Reorganization Act** to allow Native American tribes to own land, and the **Soil Conservation and Domestic Allotment Act** to help farmers.

Congress also created a variety of new agencies to provide immediate relief and a long-term plan for recovery. These agencies included the **Second Agricultural Adjustment Administration,** the **United States Housing Authority,** and the **Works Progress**

Administration (WPA). Labor organizations such as the newly formed **Congress of Industrial Workers** received a boost from the **Wagner Act** and the **Fair Labor Standards Act.**

THE COURT-PACKING SCHEME

Still, as the Great Depression entered its sixth year, Roosevelt faced an increasing amount of opposition to his New Deal. Aging, conservative Supreme Court justices, for example, struck down the National Industrial Recovery Act in *Schechter v. United States* in 1935 and the first Agricultural Adjustment Administration in *Butler v. United States* in 1936.

In 1937, Roosevelt asked Congress to allow him to add as many as six new Supreme Court justices (bringing the total number to fifteen) and to give him the power to force justices over the age of seventy to retire. This move was meant to effectively "stack the deck" in the Supreme Court to prevent the Court from striking down any more New Deal legislation. The American people, Republicans, and even some conservative members of the president's own party saw right through this **"court-packing scheme"** and were rightly outraged by it.

THE END OF THE NEW DEAL

The **"Roosevelt Recession"** of 1937 contributed to the president's plummeting popularity. Roosevelt bowed to pressure from conservatives and scaled back deficit spending in 1937, believing that the worst of the depression was over and recovery was well under way. In reality, though, the depression was far from over, and the economy was not ready to stand on its own. Without any federal support, the economy crashed again and put millions of people on the streets once more.

When this new recession hit, Roosevelt pointed fingers at everyone but himself, even though it was likely that he had caused the recession with his own policies. Americans ended up voting many New Dealers from Congress out of office in the midterm elections of 1938. Freshman Republicans then passed the **Hatch Act** of 1939 to reform national elections and weaken the Democratic Party's power over poorer Americans, who had relied heavily on New Deal handouts. With few supporters left in Congress, the New Deal was essentially dead. It would not be until the United States entered **World War II** in December 1941 that industry would recover and the economy would truly turn around.

SUMMARY OF EVENTS

Key People & Terms

People

Calvin Coolidge

A conservative from Massachusetts who became the thirtieth U.S. president upon the death of **Warren G. Harding** in 1923. In 1924, Coolidge was elected president in his own right, but in 1928 he declined an offer to run again. Like both his predecessor, Harding, and his successor, **Herbert Hoover**, Coolidge's policy was to sweep away the remnants of progressive legislation and reward big business instead.

Warren G. Harding

The twenty-ninth U.S. president, whose election in 1920 brought about a decade of **conservatism** and benefits for **big business**. Harding's isolationist stance also stifled former president Woodrow Wilson's hopes to have the United States join the **League of Nations**. Under Harding, Congress passed the **Esch-Cummins Transportation Act** and the **Fordney-McCumber Tariff**, and the United States signed the **Five-Power Naval Treaty**, the **Four-Power Treaty**, and the **Nine-Power Treaty** for disarmament and the maintenance of the status quo in East Asia. Harding's term was marred by scandal, most notably the 1923 **Teapot Dome scandal**. Harding died that same year, however, before he was fully implicated.

Herbert Hoover

A former engineer and millionaire who became the thirty-first U.S. president in 1928. Although Hoover had a reputation as a humanitarian for his relief efforts in **World War I**, he proved completely unprepared for the task of guiding the nation out of the **Great Depression**. After the **stock market crash** of 1929, Hoover encouraged Americans not to panic and promised there would be no recession. He refused to act on a federal level, taking the **laissez-faire** stance that it was not the government's job to interfere with the economy, even after millions of Americans lost their jobs and homes. Many historians believe that Hoover might have been able to curb the severity of the Great Depression had he chosen to act.

JOHN MAYNARD KEYNES

A British economist in the early twentieth century who believed that deficit spending during recessions and depressions could revive national economies. Keynes's theories went untested until **Franklin Delano Roosevelt** applied them in the **New Deal** to bring the United States out of the Great Depression. The success of the New Deal converted Democrats to **Keynesian**-minded policy makers for the next several decades.

FRANKLIN DELANO ROOSEVELT

A distant cousin of former president **Theodore Roosevelt** who served as governor of New York before becoming the thirty-second U.S. president in 1933. Roosevelt's main goal was to end the **Great Depression**. His **New Deal** programs and policies focused on immediate relief, long-term recovery, and reform in order to revive the economy. Despite the fact that he was usually wheelchair-bound (he was stricken with polio as a child), his optimism and charm did much to convince Americans that they had "nothing to fear but fear itself." After the depression, Roosevelt successfully led the United States through **World War II**, was reelected to an unprecedented fourth term in office, and died while still in office on April 12, 1945.

TERMS

AGRICULTURAL ADJUSTMENT ADMINISTRATION (AAA)

An administration created by Congress in 1933 to help destitute farmers. The AAA reset prices for agricultural commodities at their high, pre–World War I prices and paid farmers subsidies to cut production.

"BONUS ARMY"

A group of 20,000 disgruntled World War I veterans who marched on Washington, D.C., in 1932 to cash in on the army bonuses Congress promised to pay them by 1945. When Congress refused, the "Bonus Army" set up a large shantytown in the middle of the capital. **Herbert Hoover** eventually ordered federal troops to forcibly remove the veterans in what became known as the **"Battle of Anacostia Flats."** Hoover's actions to squelch the "army" proved to be a fatal political error and convinced many Americans to vote for **Franklin Delano Roosevelt** in the election later that year.

CIVILIAN CONSERVATION CORPS (CCC)

Body created by Congress in 1933 to put millions of young men to work on **conservation projects** throughout the United States. CCC workers reforested timberlands, fought forest fires, built public roads, and maintained public parks. The CCC was one of the most popular relief and recovery programs of the **New Deal**.

CRASH OF 1929

The massive crash of the U.S. **stock market** on **"Black Tuesday,"** October 29, 1929. The crash occurred after American investors dumped more than 16 million shares in one day. Within two months, more than $60 billion had been lost. The crash was the primary catalyst for the **Great Depression**.

DAWES PLAN

A plan created by Calvin Coolidge's vice president, **Charles Dawes**, to save the European economy and enrich the United States by adjusting the payment of Germany's **war reparations** from World War I. The Dawes Plan called for private American banks to loan Germany the money to pay off the billions of dollars in reparations owed to France and Britain. The English and French would then use the money to pay off war debts owed to the U.S. government. The scheme worked until the **Crash of 1929**, when American banks no longer wanted to loan Germany money.

EIGHTEENTH AMENDMENT

A constitutional amendment, ratified in 1919, that banned the consumption, sale, and manufacture of alcohol. Congress supplemented the amendment with the **Volstead Act**, which created the **Prohibition Bureau**. Prohibition remained in effect for fourteen years, until it was repealed in 1933 by the ratification of the **Twenty-First Amendment**.

EMERGENCY BANKING RELIEF ACT

A bill passed by Congress in March 1933 to give President **Franklin Delano Roosevelt** power to regulate the banking system and foreign exchange. Congress passed the act, which was the first piece of **New Deal** legislation, after Roosevelt declared a national banking holiday.

EMERGENCY QUOTA ACT

An act passed in 1921 to establish national yearly quotas for **immigration**. The act limited the total number of immigrants admitted annually from each country to 3 percent of the number of persons from that country living in the United States in 1910.

When this act failed to stem the influx of southern and eastern Europeans, it was repealed and replaced by the even more restrictive **Immigration Act of 1924.**

FAIR LABOR STANDARDS ACT
A bill passed in 1938 to establish a national minimum wage and a forty-hour workweek for workers employed by companies conducting interstate commerce. The **Fair Labor Standards Act** was one of the last pieces of **Second New Deal** legislation.

FEDERAL DEPOSIT INSURANCE CORPORATION (FDIC)
A corporation created as a result of the 1933 **Glass-Steagall Banking Reform Act** to protect individual savings accounts. The FDIC eliminated fly-by-night banks that had plagued the South and West for over a century and restored public confidence in the banking system. The FDIC was one of the main New Deal programs designed to reform the financial sector of the economy.

FEDERAL EMERGENCY RELIEF ADMINISTRATION (FERA)
An administration that Roosevelt and Congress created during the **First Hundred Days** to provide immediate economic relief. Unlike **Herbert Hoover's Reconstruction Finance Corporation**, FERA distributed grants—not loans—to state governments and individuals.

GLASS-STEAGALL BANKING REFORM ACT
An act passed in 1933 to bar U.S. banks from underwriting stocks and bonds. The act also created the **Federal Deposit Insurance Corporation (FDIC)**. Unlike the **Emergency Banking Relief Act,** the Glass-Steagall Act was aimed at providing long-term reform.

HATCH ACT
An act passed by the conservative Congress in 1939 to curb the Democrats' ability to control elections with federal handouts. The law forbade most public servants from participating in political campaigns and prohibited Americans who received federal handouts from contributing to political campaigns. Moreover, the law blocked the use of federal funds in reelection campaigns.

IMMIGRATION ACT OF 1924
A 1924 bill that reduced the national immigration quota for each foreign country from 3 percent of the number of persons from that country living in the United States in 1910 to 2 percent of the number of persons from that country living in the United States in 1890. Because so few immigrants from southern and eastern Europe had

KEY PEOPLE & TERMS

come to the United States before 1900, the act effectively barred immigration from Italy, Poland, and the Balkans.

INDIAN REORGANIZATION ACT

An act passed in 1934 to permit Native American tribal councils to own land. The **Indian Reorganization Act** reversed the 1887 **Dawes Severalty Act**, and although it was only a partial success, it did alter federal government relations with America's Native American tribes.

NINETEENTH AMENDMENT

A constitutional amendment ratified in 1920 to grant **women** the right to vote. Not surprisingly, the number of voters in the presidential election later that year nearly doubled compared to the numbers from the election of 1916.

PUBLIC WORKS ADMINISTRATION (PWA)

A government administration that **Franklin Delano Roosevelt** and Congress formed in 1933 to create new jobs, improve the nation's infrastructure, and provide unemployment relief. Part of the **First New Deal**, the PWA was very similar to the **Works Progress Administration** of the **Second New Deal**.

RED SCARE

The period immediately after the **Russian Revolution** of 1917 in which Americans feared that a similar Communist revolution might happen on U.S. soil. In 1919 and 1920, Americans became panicked and paranoid, convinced that communists were hiding and conspiring everywhere in the country. Hundreds of **American Communist Party** and **Socialist Party** members were arrested. Also, union members, who would strike and seek the right to collectively bargain with their employers, were seen as especially suspicious. As a result, unions began to shrink in number, because many labor organizers were arrested. Even those Americans who criticized the government were sometimes thrown in prison.

"ROOSEVELT RECESSION"

A 1937 recession caused by **Franklin Delano Roosevelt**'s decision to cut back on deficit spending before the Great Depression was really over. The Roosevelt Recession put millions of Americans back on the streets and contributed to the American people's loss of confidence in the president and his **New Deal** policy.

Sacco-Vanzetti Trial

The 1921 trial of Italian immigrants **Niccola Sacco** and **Bartolomeo Vanzetti**, both self-proclaimed atheists and anarchists, who were accused of murder, found guilty, and executed, largely because of their ethnicity and Communist leanings. Although historians have concluded that the men probably did in fact commit the murder, their conviction had little to do with hard evidence and more to do with the anti-immigrant and antisocialist sentiments of the day.

Schechter v. United States

A 1935 case in which the conservative Supreme Court ruled that the **National Recovery Act** was unconstitutional on the grounds that the federal government had no business controlling **intrastate commerce** (or commerce that happens within a state's boundaries). The ruling, along with the ruling in *Butler v. United States* the following year, prompted President **Franklin Delano Roosevelt** to devise his ill-fated **court-packing scheme**.

Scopes Monkey Trial

An infamous 1925 trial that dramatically played out the debate between **Christian fundamentalism** and **Charles Darwin**'s theories of **evolution** and **natural selection**. In the trial, a high school biology teacher, **John T. Scopes**, was accused of flouting a Tennessee ban on the teaching of evolution. Although Scopes technically lost the case, fundamentalists came away looking ridiculous, especially after confusing and contradictory answers given by former politician and "Bible expert" **William Jennings Bryan**.

Second Agricultural Adjustment Administration

A body created in 1938 that paid **subsidies** to farmers to cut farm acreage in order to curb overproduction. Congress created the Second Agricultural Adjustment Administration after the Supreme Court declared the First Administration unconstitutional.

Smoot-Hawley Tariff

A tariff passed by Congress and **Herbert Hoover** in 1930 that raised the tax on foreign goods to nearly 60 percent. The Smoot-Hawley Tariff crippled the American and international economies at a time when the world badly needed trade—not trade protection—to pull out of the widespread economic depression that was rapidly unfolding into the **Great Depression**.

Social Security Act

A 1935 act that established pensions for the elderly, handicapped, and unemployed. The Social Security Act completely changed the way Americans thought about work and proved to be one of the most significant pieces of legislation in the **Second New Deal**.

Soil Conservation and Domestic Allotment Act

A bill passed by Congress in 1936 (as part of the **Second New Deal**) that paid farmers subsidies to grow fewer crops in order to curb overproduction. The act also gave farmers extra subsidies to plant crops that would put nutrients back in the soil, in lieu of nutrient-depleting crops such as wheat.

Teapot Dome Scandal

A scandal during **Warren G. Harding**'s presidency in which the secretaries of the interior and the navy took large bribes to let a private company drill oil on federal lands near the town of **Teapot Dome**, Wyoming. Harding himself was implicated in the scheme but died before any charges could be filed. The scandal was the most famous of the many that surfaced during Harding's term.

Tennessee Valley Authority (TVA)

A government agency specifically created to help the **Tennessee River valley**, which was one of the poorest regions of the United States during and prior to the **Great Depression**. The TVA worked to modernize the region and reduce unemployment by hiring local workers to construct dams and hydroelectric power plants. The TVA, though a success, was not without controversy: electric companies denounced the agency for producing cheap electricity and decreasing profits, and conservative Americans saw government-produced electricity as a step toward socialism. Still, the TVA improved the quality of life in the region so much that similar projects soon sprang up in the West and South. Within a decade, many major U.S. rivers had dams and hydroelectric power plants to provide electricity and jobs.

Twenty-First Amendment

A constitutional amendment ratified in 1933 to repeal the **Eighteenth Amendment**, which had initiated **Prohibition**.

Wagner Act

A 1935 act of Congress that legalized labor unions' right to organize and bargain collectively. Also known as the **National Labor Relations**

Act, the passage of the act was a momentous day for American laborers and initiated a series of strikes throughout the country. The act also helped the **Congress of Industrial Organizations** to form in 1935.

WORKS PROGRESS ADMINISTRATION (WPA)

A government administration created in 1935 to hire over 10 million American men to construct **public works projects** such as roads, bridges, and public buildings. The WPA, one of the most significant programs created during the **Second New Deal,** helped provide immediate relief for many Americans during the Great Depression.

SUMMARY & ANALYSIS

THE POLITICS OF CONSERVATISM: 1920–1928

EVENTS

1920	Nineteenth Amendment is ratified
	Congress Passes the Esch-Cummins Transportation Act
	Warren G. Harding is elected president
1922	Five-Power, Nine-Power, and Four-Power treaties signed
	Congress passes Fordney-McCumber Tariff
1923	Teapot Dome scandal
	Adkins v. Children's Hospital
	Harding dies in office; Calvin Coolidge becomes president
1924	Calvin Coolidge is elected president
	Dawes Plan
1926	Coolidge sends American forces to Nicaragua
1928	Kellogg-Briand Pact is signed
	Herbert Hoover is elected president

KEY PEOPLE

Warren G. Harding 29th U.S. president; was involved in Teapot Dome scandal but died before being implicated

Calvin Coolidge 30th U.S. president; took office upon Harding's death in 1923; advocated conservative policies

Herbert Hoover 31st U.S. president; elected in 1928

HARDING AND THE ELECTION OF 1920

After the end of **World War I**, President **Woodrow Wilson**, unable to convince Republicans in the Senate to ratify the **Treaty of Versailles**, stated emphatically that the American people should settle the issue of the **League of Nations** in the presidential election of 1920. Democrats and Republicans both nominated Ohioans, **James Cox** on the Democratic, pro-League platform and Senator **Warren G. Harding** on the Republican ticket. Harding hoped to attract both conservative and liberal votes by skirting the troublesome issue of the League of Nations on a platform neither for the League nor against it. Imprisoned labor leader **Eugene V. Debs** also ran on the **Socialist Party** ticket and did surprisingly well considering his imprisonment and the anticommunist sentiment of the day.

Harding's noncommittal stance paid off on Election Day, as he defeated Cox by a margin of more than 7 million popular votes and won 404 electoral votes to Cox's 127. As a result of the 1920 ratification of the **Nineteenth Amendment**, the election was the first time women had voted in a national election in American history.

PRO-BUSINESS POLICIES

Harding's election meant big bucks for **big business**. The antitrust gains made by Wilsonian **progressives** went out the door as a new age dawned for fat-cat tycoons and good old boys in the Republican Party. Ironically, though, many of Harding's pro-business policies hurt the American economy in the long run. First, the sudden free-for-all in the market led to speculation and corruption. Speculators began using **future earnings** on the stocks they owned—money they did not even have yet—to buy new stocks, a process known as **"buying on margin."** This overspeculation, along with widespread corruption and faulty international finances, eventually led to the stock market **crash of 1929**.

Moreover, the steep **Fordney-McCumber Tariff** prevented Europe from exporting goods to the United States to boost its economy after the war. Europe was deeply in debt and needed to sell goods to American consumers to pay off loans owed to the U.S. government. Harding's new tariff sparked an international tariff war that brought international trade to a virtual standstill.

HARDING'S CONSERVATISM

Conservatism flourished under Harding as the president distributed rewards to big business and limited benefits for average American workers. In 1923, for example, the Supreme Court ruled in *Adkins v. Children's Hospital* that women workers did not merit special labor protection from the government, because they were now enfranchised and could theoretically protect themselves. This decision effectively reversed the previous 1908 *Muller v. Oregon* ruling.

Meanwhile, Congress passed the **Esch-Cummins Transportation Act** in 1920, which deregulated railroads, putting their control back into the hands of plutocratic owners. In 1922, Harding and Congress also passed the **Fordney-McCumber Tariff**, which drove taxes on foreign goods up to almost 40 percent to protect American industry. Such conservative measures, combined with the federal government's new willingness to break **strikes** using force, caused a drastic drop in **labor union** membership throughout the country.

SUMMARY & ANALYSIS

INTERNATIONAL DISARMAMENT

Harding's foreign policy was likewise dominated by conservatism. Although Secretary of State **Charles Evans Hughes** opened negotiations for American rights to oil in the Middle East, the president focused mainly on maintaining the status quo and reducing American involvement abroad.

In 1922, the United States convinced Britain and Japan to sign the **Five-Power Naval Treaty**, which would reduce the number of battleships each country had in the Pacific to a ratio of 5:5:3, respectively. The United States and Britain promised not to fortify their Pacific bases but allowed Japan to fortify its bases to counter the battleship imbalance. The United States also signed the **Four-Power Treaty** with Britain, Japan, and France, which forbade the countries from acquiring new possessions in the Pacific, while the **Nine-Power Treaty** upheld John Hay's old **Open Door policy** in China.

DEVELOPMENTS IN GERMANY AND JAPAN

During this period of American isolationism, events were unfolding around the world that would have catastrophic consequences later on. In **Germany** during the 1920s and during the Great Depression, a man by the name of **Adolf Hitler** began to gather a tremendous political following as he proposed solutions to Germany's economic problems and promised to make the Fatherland strong again. Desperate Germans clung to Hitler's rhetoric, as **hyperinflation** was causing the German mark to fall in value literally by the minute. This inflation in Germany became so extreme that prices of meals at restaurants would increase significantly between the time patrons started eating and the time they finished.

Japan, meanwhile, was capitalizing on the Five-Power and Four-Power treaties by strengthening its presence in East Asia. It had had its eyes on the **Manchuria** region of China for years and was waiting for the right moment to take it.

THE TEAPOT DOME SCANDAL

At home, Harding's deregulation of big business led to government scandal and corruption that tainted his presidency. The most notorious scandal during his term was the **Teapot Dome scandal** of 1923, which erupted after a private company bribed the secretaries of the interior and navy to overlook the illegal drilling of oil from government lands in Teapot Dome, Wyoming. Harding himself was implicated in the scandal but died later that year before anyone made any serious accusations. He was replaced by the even more conservative Vice President **Calvin Coolidge**.

THE ELECTION OF 1924

A year later, the American people elected Coolidge president in yet another three-way election. Coolidge's opponents were Democrat **John W. Davis** and the recently revamped **Progressive Party**'s nominee, **Robert La Follette**. La Follette campaigned for more debt relief and protection from big business and a constitutional amendment to revoke the Supreme Court's power of judicial review. Coolidge won a landslide victory, though La Follette did receive thirteen electoral votes.

THE DAWES PLAN

With business burgeoning at home, Coolidge focused on foreign policy. At the time, **Germany** was suffering from extreme hyperinflation in the aftermath of World War I due to unrealistic French and British demands for **war reparations**. In 1924, Coolidge and Vice President **Charles Dawes** drafted the **Dawes Plan** to assist Germany by setting up a new timetable for its reparations payments.

Under the plan, U.S. banks issued long-term loans to the German government; France and Britain then used the German reparations to pay back the billions of dollars they themselves had borrowed from the United States during the war. For a time, the system worked: Germany had a little breathing room, while France and England were able to maintain their credit by paying off war debts to Washington. Meanwhile, American bankers reaped huge profits from the plan.

The U.S. stock market crash of 1929 (*see* The Depression Begins, *p. 5*), however, changed everything. Suddenly, the United States needed the money it was being paid as badly as the other countries involved in the plan, and U.S. banks refused to issue any more private loans to Germany. Germany, therefore, could not pay France and Britain, who then had to default on their loans to the United States. Neither American investors nor the U.S. government ever saw the money again, and the United States came away from the Dawes Plan looking like greedy backstabbers in the eyes of Europe.

THE KELLOGG-BRIAND PACT

In 1928, President Coolidge and Secretary of State **Frank B. Kellogg** touted the signing of the multinational **Kellogg-Briand Pact**, a rather naive agreement that "outlawed" war in an attempt to ensure that

World War I was the "war to end all wars." The pact specified virtually no means of enforcement and was thus effectively useless. More than anything, it was a reflection of American public sentiment during the peak of prosperity in the late 1920s: Americans began to feel that if another world war erupted, the United States should not have a part in it. Many Americans wanted a return to the neutrality and isolationism that George Washington originally advocated, leaving Europe to solve its own problems.

The Roaring Twenties and the Jazz Age: 1920–1929

Events

1920	Nineteenth Amendment is ratified
	Sinclair Lewis publishes *Main Street*
1925	F. Scott Fitzgerald publishes *The Great Gatsby*
1926	Ernest Hemingway publishes *The Sun Also Rises*
1927	Charles Lindbergh becomes first pilot to fly solo across Atlantic
	The Jazz Singer becomes first "talkie"
1929	William Faulkner publishes *The Sound and the Fury*

Key People

Henry Ford Automobile pioneer who perfected assembly-line production and invented the affordable Model T Ford

F. Scott Fitzgerald Writer whose novels and stories depicted the excitement and dislocation of the Jazz Age

Ernest Hemingway Novelist whose works typified the disillusioned voice of the post–World War I Lost Generation

The "Roaring Twenties"

Culturally and socially, the **Roaring Twenties** were a heady time of rapid change, artistic innovation, and high-society antics. Popular culture roared to life as the economy boomed. New technologies, soaring business profits, and higher wages allowed more and more Americans to purchase a wide range of consumer goods. Prosperity also provided Americans with more leisure time, and as play soon became the national pastime, literature, film, and music caught up to document the times.

The Second Industrial Revolution

Much of the impetus for this modernization came from America's so-called **second Industrial Revolution**, which had begun around the turn of the century. During this era, **electricity** and more advanced **machinery** made factories nearly twice as efficient as they had been under steam power in the 1800s.

Henry Ford and the Automobile

Perhaps the greatest increase in efficiency came when **Henry Ford** perfected the **assembly-line** production method, which enabled factories to churn out large quantities of a variety of new technological wonders, such as radios, telephones, refrigerators, washing machines, and cars. The increasing availability of such **consumer goods** pushed modernization forward, and the U.S. economy began to shift away from heavy industry toward the production of these commodities.

The **automobile** quickly became the symbol of the new America. Although Americans did not invent the car, they certainly perfected it. Much of the credit for this feat went to Ford and his assembly-line method, which transformed the car from a luxury item into a necessity for modern living. By the mid-1920s, even many working-class families could afford a brand-new **Model T** Ford, priced at just over $250. Increasing demand for the automobile in turn trickled down to many other industries. The demand for oil, for example, boomed, and oil prospectors set up new wells in Texas and the Southwest practically overnight. Newer and smoother roads were constructed across America, dotted with new service stations. Change came so rapidly that by 1930, almost one in three Americans owned cars.

THE BIRTH OF THE SUBURBS
Its effect on the U.S. economy aside, the automobile also changed American life immeasurably. Cars most directly affected the way that Americans moved around, but this change also affected the way that Americans lived and spent their free time. Trucks provided faster modes of transport for crops and perishable foods and therefore improved the quality and freshness of purchasable food. Perhaps most important, the automobile allowed people to leave the inner city and live elsewhere without changing jobs. During the 1920s, more people purchased houses in new residential communities within an easy drive of the metropolitan centers. After a decade, these **suburbs** had grown exponentially, making the car more of a necessity than ever.

MODERN U.S. CITIES
American cities changed drastically during the 1920s because of factors above and beyond those related to the automobile. First, the decade saw millions of people flock to the cities from country farmlands; in particular, **African Americans** fled the South for northern cities in the post–World War I black migration. **Immigrants**, especially eastern Europeans, also flooded the cities. As a result of these changes, the number of American city dwellers—those who lived in towns with a population greater than 2,500 people—came to outnumber those who lived in rural areas for the first time in U.S. history.

At the same time, new architectural techniques allowed builders to construct taller buildings. The first **skyscrapers** began dotting city skylines in the 1920s, and by 1930, several hundred buildings over twenty stories tall existed in U.S. cities.

THE AIRPLANE

Aviation developed quickly after the Wright brothers' first sustained powered flight in 1903, and by the 1920s, **airplanes** were becoming a significant part of American life. Several passenger airline companies, subsidized by U.S. Mail contracts, sprang to life, allowing wealthier citizens to travel across the country in a matter of hours rather than days or weeks. In 1927, stunt flyer **Charles Lindbergh** soared to international fame when he made the first solo flight across the Atlantic Ocean (from New York to Paris) in his single-engine plane, the *Spirit of St. Louis*. His achievement gave an enormous boost to the growing aviation industry.

RADIO AND THE JAZZ AGE

Another influential innovation of the time was the **radio**, which entertained and brought Americans together like nothing else had before. Electricity became more readily available throughout the decade, and by 1930, most American households had radio receivers. The advertising industry blossomed as companies began to deliver their sales pitches via the airwaves to thousands of American families who gathered together nightly to listen to popular comedy programs, news, speeches, sporting events, and music.

In particular, **jazz** music became incredibly popular. Originating in black communities in New Orleans around the turn of the century, jazz slowly moved its way north and became a national phenomenon thanks to the radio. Along with new music came "scandalous" new dances such as the Charleston and the jitterbug.

HOLLYWOOD AND "TALKIES"

The Hollywood **motion picture industry** also emerged during the 1920s. Although movies were nothing new to Americans, as silent films had enjoyed widespread popularity during the previous decade, the first **"talkies"** brought actors' voices into theaters and kicked the moviemaking business into high gear. Glamorous actors and actresses soon enjoyed the status of royalty and came to dominate American pop culture.

LOST GENERATION LITERATURE

While pop culture burgeoned, a new generation of postwar American authors penned a flurry of new poems, plays, and novels. In 1920, **F. Scott Fitzgerald** gained almost instant fame when he glamorized the new youth culture in *This Side of Paradise*. Five years later, he followed up his first success with the critically acclaimed novel *The Great Gatsby*. **William Faulkner** became the new voice of the South with novels such as *The Sound and the Fury* (1929). World War I veteran **Ernest Hemingway** published the antiwar novels *The Sun Also Rises* (1926) and *A Farewell to Arms* (1929).

Other notable writers and poets of the era included **T. S. Eliot**, **Sherwood Anderson**, **Sinclair Lewis**, and playwright **Eugene O'Neill**. Together, these writers, disillusioned with war and society, became known as the **Lost Generation**. Black culture in the North also flourished throughout the years of the **Harlem Renaissance**, during which writers such as **Langston Hughes** and **Zora Neale Hurston** created a new tradition in African-American poetry, fiction, and scholarship.

WOMEN'S SUFFRAGE AND THE SEXUAL REVOLUTION

The booming twenties also brought more rights and freedoms for **women**. In 1920, the **Nineteenth Amendment** granted American women the right to vote. Just as important, more women gained financial independence as the number of women in the workforce skyrocketed. Approximately 15 percent of women were employed by 1930. Although they were generally confined to "traditional" women's jobs such as secretarial work and teaching, the new financial freedom that these jobs afforded opened the doors to increased social mobility for women.

As women's rights increased, so too did social freedoms. A new symbol of the Jazz Age emerged: the image of the short-haired, short-skirted, independent-minded, and sexually liberated **"flapper"** woman who lived life in the fast lane. Soon, the flapper came to represent everything modern in 1920s America. With this new image of women, a sexual revolution followed as attitudes toward sex changed and birth control became widely accepted and available.

THE CONSERVATIVE BACKLASH: 1919–1929

EVENTS

1919	Eighteenth Amendment (Prohibition) is ratified Congress passes Volstead Act
1920	Red Scare
1921	Sacco-Vanzetti trial Congress passes Emergency Quota Act
1924	Congress passes Immigration Act of 1924
1925	Scopes Monkey Trial

PROHIBITION

At the same time that the liberalism of the Jazz Age flourished, so did a movement of **social conservatism**—perhaps the most identifiable example of which was **Prohibition**. Ratified in 1919, the **Eighteenth Amendment** to the Constitution outlawed the sale, manufacture, and consumption of alcohol. Reformers had been trying to pass prohibition laws since the 1830s and 1840s but had never before achieved such success. Congress also passed the **Volstead Act**, which established the federal Prohibition Bureau to enforce the amendment. Enforcement of the ban on alcohol proved difficult as **bootleggers** continued to produce and sell liquor illegally, and drinking continued to take place in underground **speakeasies**. The Prohibition experiment lasted only fourteen years, as Congress repealed it by ratifying the **Twenty-First Amendment** in 1933.

POLITICAL DIVIDES AND ORGANIZED CRIME

Although Prohibition did significantly reduce the national consumption of alcohol, it alienated a huge portion of Americans—many of them European immigrants—who were accustomed to drinking regularly. The law also sparked intense debate, as "wet" politicians (often Democrats) decried the hypocrisy of the "experiment" while "dry" politicians (generally Republicans) preached the new law's moral and social benefits.

Prohibition also brought negative consequences to American society, such as the birth of **organized crime**. Big-name **gangsters** such as **Al Capone** illegally produced and distributed alcohol, bribed local police forces to turn a blind eye to their illegal activities, and became extremely powerful. Federal agents in the newly formed

Prohibition Bureau, who were grossly understaffed and overworked, could do little to stop the gangsters' activities.

NEW RESTRICTIONS ON IMMIGRATION

Many Americans stood firmly against immigration during the 1920s. Although **nativist** groups such as the **Know-Nothings** and the **American Protective Association** had been around since the 1800s, Congress had rarely given in to these groups and had done little to stem the flow of immigrants into the United States. All this changed in 1921, however, when Congress passed the **Emergency Quota Act** in response to the unceasing wave of new immigrants into the country.

As its name implied, the Emergency Quota Act established a specific, unalterable number of immigrants from each country who would be allowed to enter the United States every year. Specifically, each immigrant's country of origin could send only 3 percent of the number of persons from that country who were living in the United States in 1910; all other immigrants would be shipped back to the countries from which they came. Three years later, Congress repealed the Emergency Quota Act and passed the **Immigration Act of 1924,** which changed each foreign country's annual immigrant quota to 2 percent of the number of persons from that country who were living in the United States in 1890.

In general, immigration had been a boon to the rapidly expanding U.S. economy during the nineteenth century, as immigrants from Ireland, Germany, and southern Europe had provided invaluable labor in city factories. The Emergency Quota Act and the Immigration Act of 1924, however, effectively slammed the door shut on the bulk of new immigrants. The effect was enormous and reduced the number of yearly arrivals by about 500,000 annually—blocking almost all southern and eastern Europeans. The number of immigrants from northern and western Europe, on the other hand, remained relatively steady, between 150,000 and 200,000 per year. These laws implemented the first severe limitations on immigration after nearly a century without much restriction.

THE RED SCARE

Congress passed these new restrictive immigration laws in part because of the growing fear of **socialism** that was spreading through southern and eastern Europe. After Russia collapsed to communism in the **Russian Revolution** of 1917, panic swept across the United States. In the **Red Scare** of 1919–1920, Americans became suspicious that they might fall victim to a communist plot to take over the country. The two main methods that workers' unions used to create fair labor agreements—striking and collective bargaining—came to be seen as tools of socialists and anarchists. As a result, labor unions were frowned upon and dwindled in number and size. Several hundred Americans who affiliated with the Communist and Socialist parties were arrested, as were labor organizers and others who criticized the U.S. government.

The **Socialist Party**'s growing membership in the United States was also perceived as a threat, especially since labor organizer **Eugene V. Debs** received nearly a million popular votes in the presidential election of 1920. Even though the Red Scare eventually subsided, the fear of socialism and communism in the United States never truly went away. It would eventually resurface in the 1950s and throughout the Cold War.

THE SACCO-VANZETTI TRIAL

Americans' fears of immigration and socialism coalesced in the sensational **Sacco-Vanzetti Trial** of 1921, in which Italian-born Niccola Sacco and Bartolomeo Vanzetti were tried for murder. The two also happened to be self-proclaimed atheists and anarchists, which did not win them any favor from the conservative segment of the public. Although historians have concluded that both men were most likely guilty of the crime, at the time of the trial itself, the defendants' ethnicity and communist affiliations weighed far more heavily than any hard evidence. In the end, Sacco and Vanzetti were convicted of murder and executed.

FUNDAMENTALISM VS. DARWINISM

Millions of Americans also found a renewed sense of faith during the 1920s, defending traditional interpretations of the Bible against scientific theories that challenged those traditions. **Charles Darwin**'s theories of **evolution** and **natural selection** were particularly threatening because they suggested that the world had been created over the course of millions of years—rather than seven days as the Bible stated—and that human beings were just one by-product of the evolutionary process. **Fundamentalists**, those who believed in the literal translation of the Bible, contested Darwin's theories in an extremely heated debate.

THE SCOPES MONKEY TRIAL

Nothing encapsulated the battle between fundamentalists and evolutionists better than the infamous **Scopes Monkey Trial** of 1925. In the trial, Tennessee biology teacher John T. Scopes was accused of presenting Darwin's theories to high school students, in violation of a state law that forbade the teaching of evolution and natural selection. Some of the nation's finest lawyers descended on the small town of Dayton, Tennessee, to present their arguments for the case, with numerous journalists in tow. Defense lawyer **Clarence Darrow** and fundamentalist prosecutor **William Jennings Bryan** (of late-1800s populism fame) provided the highlight of the trial when Darrow made Bryan look ridiculous on the witness stand. Although Scopes was ultimately found guilty and fined for his transgression, the fact that Bryan and his team came across as silly and unreasonable ended up bolstering the evolutionists' side of the debate.

THE REEMERGENCE OF THE KU KLUX KLAN

The growing Protestant conservatism of the day also manifested itself in the swelling membership of the white supremacist group the **Ku Klux Klan**. Although the Klan of the 1920s was still ultraconservative and militant, it looked quite different from the Klan of the Reconstruction era and the Gilded Age. Whereas the Klan of the past had formed in the South to suppress blacks' civil liberties, the new KKK was a national movement against not only blacks but also Catholics, Jews, alcohol, immigration, communism, and even birth control. Membership jumped to several million by the middle of the 1920s.

The newer, bigger, angrier KKK was also a significant part of the fundamentalist movement during the first half of the decade. Though the Klan existed primarily to intimidate minority groups, it also served as a social organization for conservatives, especially in the South and Midwest. Klansmen and -women would organize picnics, parades, parties, and festivals for members to celebrate and discuss politics. Membership dwindled, however, after numerous scandals were uncovered within the organization. In addition, other conservative movements of the 1920s began to achieve many of the Klan's goals: "undesirable" immigrants were being turned away, Prohibition was in effect, communists were being persecuted, fundamentalists had won the Scopes Monkey Trial, and the economy was "roaring."

The Onset of the Depression: 1928–1932

Events

1928	Herbert Hoover is elected president
1929	Stock market crashes
1932	Reconstruction Finance Corporation is created Congress passes Norris–La Guardia Anti-Injunction Act "Bonus Army" camps out in Washington, D.C. Franklin D. Roosevelt is elected president

Key People

Herbert Hoover 31st U.S. president; failed to provide federal relief after Crash of 1929 and adhered firmly to laissez-faire economic policy

Franklin Delano Roosevelt 32nd U.S. president; elected in 1932 after serving as governor of New York

The Election of 1928

Despite the booming U.S. economy of the late 1920s, **Calvin Coolidge** decided not to run for president again. In his place, Republicans nominated the president's handpicked successor, popular World War I humanitarian administrator **Herbert Hoover**, to continue America's prosperity. Democrats chose New York Governor **Alfred E. Smith** on an anti-Prohibition platform. Hoover won with ease, with 444 electoral votes to Smith's 87 and with a margin of more than 6 million popular votes.

The Crash of 1929

Soon after Hoover took office, the good times and successful run of the bull market came to an abrupt halt. Stiffer competition with Britain for foreign investment spurred **speculators** to dump American **stocks** and securities in the late summer of 1929. By late October, it was clear that the bull had been grabbed by the horns, and an increasing number of Americans pulled their money out of the stock market. The **Dow Jones Industrial Average** fell steadily over a ten-day period, finally crashing on October 29, 1929. On this so-called **Black Tuesday**, investors panicked and dumped an unprecedented 16 million shares.

The rampant practice of **buying on margin** (*see* The Politics of Conservatism, *p. 17*), which had damaged Americans' credit, made the effects of the stock market crash worse. As a result, within one month, American investors had lost tens of billions of dollars. Although the 1929 stock market crash was certainly the catalyst for the Great Depression, it was not the sole cause. Historians still debate exactly why the Great Depression was so severe, but they generally agree that it was the result of a confluence of factors.

CONSUMER GOODS AND CREDIT

Ever since the turn of the century, the foundation of the American economy had been shifting from heavy industry to **consumer products**. In other words, whereas most of America's wealth in the late 1800s had come from producing iron, steel, coal, and oil, the economy of the early 1900s was based on manufacturing automobiles, radios, and myriad other items that Americans could buy for use in their own homes.

As Americans jumped on the consumer bandwagon, an increasing number of people began purchasing goods on **credit**, promising to pay for items later rather than up front. When the economic bubble of the 1920s burst, debtors were unable to pay up, and creditors were forced to absorb millions of dollars in bad loans. Policy makers found it difficult to end the depression's vicious circle in this new consumer economy: Americans were unable to buy goods without jobs, yet factories were unable to provide jobs because Americans were not able to buy anything the factories produced.

MARGIN BUYING

Consumer goods were not the only commodities Americans bought on credit; **buying stocks on margin** had become very popular during the Roaring Twenties. In margin buying, an individual could purchase a share of a company's stock and then use the promise of that share's future earnings to buy more shares. Unfortunately, many people abused the system to invest huge sums of imaginary money that existed only on paper.

OVERPRODUCTION IN FACTORIES

Overproduction in manufacturing was also an economic concern during the era leading up to the depression. During the 1920s, factories produced an increasing amount of popular consumer goods in an effort to match demand. Although factory output soared as more companies utilized new machines to increase production, wages for American workers remained basically the same, so demand did not keep up with supply. Eventually, the price of goods plummeted when there were more goods in the market than people could afford to buy. The effect was magnified after the stock market crash, when people had even less money to spend.

OVERPRODUCTION ON FARMS

Farmers faced a similar overproduction crisis. Soaring debt forced many farmers to plant an increasing amount of profitable cash crops such as **wheat**. Although wheat depleted the soil of nutrients and eventually made it unsuitable for planting, farmers were desperate for income and could not afford to plant less profitable crops. Unfortunately, the aggregate effect of all these farmers planting wheat was a **surplus** of wheat on the market, which drove prices down and, in a vicious cycle, forced farmers to plant even more wheat the next year. Furthermore, the toll that the repeated wheat crops took on the soil contributed to the 1930s environmental disaster of the **Dust Bowl** in the West (*see* The Dust Bowl, *p. 33*).

INCOME INEQUALITY

Income inequality, which was greater in the late 1920s than in any other time in U.S. history, also contributed to the severity of the Great Depression. By the time of the stock market crash, the top 1 percent of Americans owned more than a third of all the nation's wealth, while the poorest 20 percent owned a meager 4 percent of it. There was essentially no middle class: a few Americans were rich, and the vast majority were poor or barely above the poverty line. This disparity made the depression even harder for Americans to overcome.

BAD BANKING PRACTICES

Reckless banking practices did not help the economic situation either. Many U.S. banks in the early 1900s were little better than the fly-by-night banks of the 1800s, especially in rural areas of the West and South. Because virtually no federal regulations existed to control banks, Americans had few means of protesting bad banking practices. Corruption was rampant, and most Americans had no idea what happened to their money after they handed it over to a bank. Moreover, many bankers capitalized irresponsibly on the bull market, buying stocks on margin with customers' savings. When the stock market crashed, this money simply vanished, and thousands of families lost their entire life savings in a matter of minutes. Hundreds of banks failed during the first months of the Great Depression, which produced an even greater panic and rush to withdraw private savings.

SUMMARY & ANALYSIS

A Global Depression

The aftermath of World War I in Europe also played a significant role in the downward spiral of the global economy in the late 1920s. Under the terms of the **Treaty of Versailles**, Germany owed France and England enormous **war reparations** that were virtually impossible for the country to afford. France and England, in turn, owed millions of dollars in war loans to the United States. A wave of economic downturns spread through Europe, beginning in Germany, as each country became unable to pay off its debts.

Hoover's Inaction

At first, President **Herbert Hoover** and other officials downplayed the stock market crash, claiming that the economic slump would be only temporary and that it would actually help clean up corruption and bad business practices within the system. When the situation did not improve, Hoover advocated a strict **laissez-faire** (hands-off) policy dictating that the federal government should not interfere with the economy but rather let the economy right itself. Furthermore, Hoover argued that the nation would pull out of the slump if American families merely steeled their determination, continued to work hard, and practiced self-reliance.

The Smoot-Hawley Tariff

Hoover made another serious miscalculation by signing into law the 1930 **Smoot-Hawley Tariff**, which drove the average tariff rate on imported goods up to almost 60 percent. Although the move was meant to protect American businesses, it was so punitive that it prompted retaliation from foreign nations, which in turn stopped buying American goods. This retaliation devastated American producers, who needed *any* sales—foreign or domestic—desperately. As a result, U.S. trade with Europe and other foreign nations tailed off dramatically, hurting the economy even more.

The Reconstruction Finance Corporation

When it became clear that the economy was not righting itself, Hoover held to his laissez-faire ideals and took only an indirect approach to jump-starting the economy. He created several committees in the early 1930s to look into helping American farmers and industrial corporations get back on their feet. In 1932, he approved the **Reconstruction Finance Corporation (RFC)** to provide loans to banks, insurance companies, railroads, and state governments. He hoped that federal dollars dropped into the top of the economic system would help all Americans as the money "trickled down" to the bottom. Individuals, however, could not apply for RFC loans. Hoover refused to lower steep tariffs or support any "socialistic" relief proposals such as the **Muscle Shoals Bill**, which Congress drafted to harness energy from the Tennessee River.

"HOOVERVILLES"

The economic panic caused by the 1929 crash rapidly developed into a depression the likes of which Americans had never experienced. Millions lost their jobs and homes, and many went hungry as factories fired workers in the cities to cut production and expenses. Shantytowns derisively dubbed **"Hoovervilles"** sprang up seemingly overnight in cities throughout America, filled with populations of the homeless and unemployed.

In 1932, Congress took the first small step in attempting to help American workers by passing the **Norris–La Guardia Anti-Injunction Act**, which protected labor unions' right to strike. However, the bill had little effect, given that companies were already laying off employees by the hundreds or thousands because of the worsening economy.

THE DUST BOWL

Farmers, especially those in Colorado, Oklahoma, New Mexico, Kansas, and the Texas panhandle, were hit hard by the depression. Years of farming wheat without alternating crops (which was necessary to replenish soil nutrients) had turned many fields into a thick layer of barren dust. In addition, depressed crop prices—a result of overproduction—forced many farmers off their land. Unable to grow anything, thousands of families left the **Dust Bowl** region in search of work on the west coast. The plight of these Dust Bowl migrants was made famous in **John Steinbeck**'s 1939 novel *The Grapes of Wrath*.

THE "BONUS ARMY"

Middle-aged World War I **veterans** were also among the hardest hit by the depression. In 1924, Congress had agreed to pay veterans a bonus stipend that could be collected in 1945; as the depression worsened, however, more and more veterans demanded their bonus early. When Congress refused to pay, more than 20,000 veterans formed the **"Bonus Army"** and marched on Washington, D.C., in the summer of 1932. They set up a giant, filthy Hooverville in front of the Capitol, determined not to leave until they had been paid. Pres-

SUMMARY & ANALYSIS

ident Hoover reacted by ordering General **Douglas MacArthur** (later of World War II fame) to use force to remove the veterans from the Capitol grounds. Federal troops used tear gas and fire to destroy the makeshift camp in what the press dubbed the **"Battle of Anacostia Flats."**

HOOVER'S FAILURE

Hoover's inability to recognize the severity of the Great Depression only magnified the depression's effects. Many historians and economists believe that Hoover might have been able to dampen the effects of the depression by using the federal government's authority to establish financial regulations and provide direct relief to the unemployed and homeless. However, Hoover continued to adhere rigidly to his hands-off approach. This inaction, combined with Hoover's treatment of the "Bonus Army" and his repeated arguments that Americans could get through the depression simply by buckling down and working hard, convinced Americans that he was unfit to revive the economy and destroyed his previous reputation as a great humanitarian.

THE ELECTION OF 1932

When the **election of 1932** rolled around, all eyes focused on the optimistic Democratic governor of New York, **Franklin Delano Roosevelt**. A distant cousin of former president Theodore Roosevelt, FDR promised more direct relief and assistance rather than simply benefits for big business. Republicans renominated Hoover, and the election proved to be no contest. In the end, Roosevelt won a landslide victory and carried all but six states.

THE FIRST NEW DEAL: 1933–1934

EVENTS

1932	Roosevelt is elected president
1933	First Hundred Days: Congress and Roosevelt establish many New Deal agencies, including CCC, FERA, CWA, AAA, TVA, and PWA Twenty-First Amendment is ratified
1934	Congress creates Securities and Exchange Commission (SEC)

KEY PEOPLE

Franklin Delano Roosevelt 32nd U.S. president; immediately set to work creating New Deal policies to end Great Depression upon taking office in 1933

John Maynard Keynes British economist who believed that deficit spending during recessions and depressions could revive national economies; his theories formed the basis of Roosevelt's New Deal approach

THE FIRST HUNDRED DAYS

Americans voted for **Franklin Delano Roosevelt** in 1932 on the assumption that the Democrats would dole out more federal assistance than Hoover and the Republicans had. Indeed, immediately after taking the oath of office, FDR set out to provide relief, recovery, and reform in his bundle of programs known as the **New Deal**.

Roosevelt drew much of his inspiration for the New Deal from the writings of British economist **John Maynard Keynes**, who believed that a government's deficit spending could prime the economic pump and jump-start the economy. With the support of a panicked Democratic Congress, Roosevelt created most of the **"alphabet agencies"** of the **First New Deal** within his landmark **First Hundred Days** in office.

THE BANKING ACTS

On March 6, 1933, two days after becoming president, Roosevelt declared a five-day national **bank holiday** to close banks temporarily. During Hoover's presidency, roughly 1,500 banks had closed each year, and FDR hoped that a short break would give the surviving banks time to reopen on more solid footing. Several days later, Congress passed the **Emergency Banking Relief Act**, which gave Roosevelt the power to regulate banking transactions and foreign exchange.

Several months later, Congress passed the **Glass-Steagall Banking Reform Act** to protect savings deposits. The act, in turn, created the **Federal Deposit Insurance Corporation (FDIC)**, which insured an individual's savings of up to $5,000 (today, it insures deposits of up to $100,000). The act also regulated lending policies and forbade banks from investing in the stock market. After the banking crisis was resolved, Roosevelt aired the first of his **"fireside chats"** to over 50 million radio listeners, encouraging Americans to redeposit their money in the newly opened banks.

THE CIVILIAN CONSERVATION CORPS

In March 1933, Congress created the **Civilian Conservation Corps (CCC),** which hired unemployed young men to work on environmental conservation projects throughout the country. For a wage of thirty dollars a month, men worked on flood control and reforestation projects, helped improve national parks, and built many public roads. Approximately 3 million men worked in CCC camps during the program's nine-year existence.

THE FEDERAL EMERGENCY RELIEF ADMINISTRATION

The "Hundred Days Congress" also created the **Federal Emergency Relief Administration (FERA),** in May 1933, to dole out roughly $500 million to the states. About half of this money was earmarked to bail out bankrupt state and local governments. States matched the other half (three state dollars for every one federal dollar) and distributed it directly to the people. FERA also created the **Civil Works Administration (CWA),** which helped generate temporary labor for those most in need.

THE AGRICULTURAL ADJUSTMENT ADMINISTRATION

Roosevelt also encouraged the creation of the **Agricultural Adjustment Administration (AAA)** to assist America's farmers. The AAA temporarily reset prices for farm commodities, including corn, wheat, rice, milk, cotton, and livestock, and then began subsidizing farmers to reduce production. Before the depression, many debt-ridden farmers had increased crop production in order to earn more money. Ironically, this increased production had led to overproduction, which flooded the market and drove prices down, forcing farmers to plant even more the next year in a never-ending cycle. The AAA, however, began paying farmers extra to plant less or destroy their surplus crops in order to raise prices again. Congress also passed the **Farm Credit Act** to provide loans to farmers in danger of bankruptcy.

The AAA was quite controversial, as many critics wondered why landowners rather than sharecroppers and tenant farmers were receiving federal aid. Indeed, some landowners who received aid unjustly used it to purchase farm equipment, which had the potential to eliminate farm owners' need for sharecroppers and tenant farmers entirely. Furthermore, many poorer and hungrier Americans were outraged that the government was paying farmers money to destroy perfectly edible crops in order to inflate prices. Despite these criticisms, however, the AAA did manage to raise prices to their pre–World War I highs.

The Tennessee Valley Authority

Congress also created the **Tennessee Valley Authority (TVA)**, whose goal was to modernize and reduce unemployment in the Tennessee River valley, one of the poorest and hardest-hit regions in the country. The agency hired local workers to construct a series of dams and hydroelectric power plants, which brought cheap electricity to thousands of people. The public corporation also created affordable employee housing, manufactured cheap fertilizer, and drained thousands of acres for farming.

The TVA, like the AAA, was highly controversial. Many conservatives claimed that government production of electricity was a mild form of socialism and that it disrupted market prices too much. Competing electric companies also attacked the TVA for selling cheaper electricity and lowering their profits. Still, the TVA had such a profound impact on the economy and quality of life in the Tennessee River valley region that the federal government initiated similar projects throughout the West and South. Within a decade, many major U.S. rivers were set up to produce hydroelectric power that provided both electricity and jobs.

The National Industrial Recovery Act

The 1933 **National Industrial Recovery Act** was the federal government's first attempt to revive the economy as a whole. The bill created the **National Recovery Administration (NRA)** to stimulate industrial production and improve competition by drafting corporate codes of conduct. The NRA also sought to limit production of consumer goods to drive up prices. Furthermore, the act helped set up the **Public Works Administration (PWA)** to construct public roads, bridges, and buildings. In accordance with Keynesian economic theories, Roosevelt believed that improving the public infrastructure would put more money into the economy.

Restructuring American Finance

Finally, Roosevelt also lobbied Congress to establish new regulations on the **financial sector** of the economy. After taking office, he took the country off the **gold standard**, which allowed citizens and

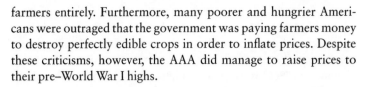

SUMMARY & ANALYSIS

foreign countries to exchange paper money for gold. To prevent people from hoarding the precious metal, the president also ordered all private gold stocks to be turned over to the U.S. Treasury in exchange for paper dollars. Congress also created the **Securities and Exchange Commission (SEC)** to regulate trading on Wall Street and curb the out-of-control speculation that had led to the Crash of 1929.

THE THREE RS AND THEIR LEGACY

Although the New Deal sometimes comes across as a cohesive package, much of the individual legislation passed during the First Hundred Days was conceived on the fly. So many special interest groups, such as big business and organized labor, were hounding the government for change that Roosevelt and Congress often felt they were being pulled in opposite directions.

Nevertheless, the New Deal policies did much to get Americans back on their feet. They not only provided **relief, recovery,** and **reform** but also drastically changed the federal government's role in politics and society. Roosevelt's successful application of Keynes's economic theories transformed the Democrats into social welfare advocates. Even decades after the Great Depression, Democratic politicians would continue fighting for more government intervention in the economy, redistribution of wealth, and aid for the neediest.

RELIEF

Much of the legislation that the Hundred Days Congress drafted doled out immediate relief for the American people that President Hoover and the Republicans had failed to provide. The Federal Emergency Relief Administration's relief assistance, for example, provided millions of Americans with enough money to make ends meet. The Civil Works Administration put the unemployed to work, and the Agricultural Adjustment Administration, the Tennessee Valley Authority, the National Recovery Administration, and the Public Works Administration kept millions of others alive as well. Americans were so relieved by the federal government's quick action that many became die-hard Democrats and Roosevelt fans. The president's optimism and can-do attitude, combined with the success of his immediate relief programs, made him almost politically untouchable during his first term.

RECOVERY

Many of the same programs designed to provide immediate relief were also geared toward long-term economic recovery. The Civilian

Conservation Corps and the Public Works Administration put millions of men to work not only to keep them employed but also to improve the national **infrastructure**. When the United States finally emerged from the Great Depression during World War II, it had hundreds of new roads and public buildings, widespread electrical power, and replenished resources for industry.

REFORM

The third goal of the New Deal policies was to reform the banking and financial sector of the economy to curb bad lending practices, poor trading techniques, and corruption. The president's decision to take the country off the gold standard proved to be a smart move because it boosted people's confidence in the U.S. dollar. The Federal Deposit Insurance Corporation, created under the Glass-Steagall Act, eliminated untrustworthy banks that had plagued the country for more than a century. Once Americans became confident that their funds would be safe, the number of bank deposits surged. Likewise, the Securities and Exchange Commission in 1934, which weeded out bad investment habits, gave Americans more confidence in the stock market.

THE GOOD NEIGHBOR POLICY

Although foreign policy often got lost in the shuffle amid the domestic economic concerns of the New Deal, Roosevelt did create a major international initiative with Latin America in the **Good Neighbor Policy** of 1933 and 1934. As part of the initiative, Roosevelt embarked on a tour of the region; signed new, friendlier treaties with several Latin American countries; pledged to avoid military intervention in Latin America; and shunned the (Theodore) Roosevelt Corollary to the Monroe Doctrine by withdrawing troops from several countries.

SUMMARY & ANALYSIS

THE SECOND NEW DEAL: 1935–1938

EVENTS

1934	Indian Reorganization Act (IRA)
1935	Works Progress Administration (WPA) National Labor Relations Act (Wagner Act) Social Security Act
1936	Soil Conservation and Domestic Allotment Act Roosevelt is reelected
1937	United States Housing Authority (USHA)
1938	Second Agricultural Adjustment Act Fair Labor Standards Act

KEY PEOPLE

Franklin Delano Roosevelt 32nd U.S. president; reelected in 1936; brought Second New Deal programs and policy through Congress

Huey P. Long Louisiana senator who criticized New Deal for not doing enough to help American people; was assassinated before he could seriously challenge Roosevelt

Father Charles Coughlin Catholic priest in Michigan and outspoken New Deal critic; blamed Crash of 1929 on wealthy financiers and Jews; wanted federal government to take over entire banking system

Alfred M. Landon Kansas governor who ran against FDR on anti–New Deal Republican ticket in election of 1936

THE SECOND NEW DEAL

The **Second New Deal**—the legislation that Roosevelt and Congress passed between 1935 and 1938—was strikingly different from the First New Deal in certain ways. Perhaps most important, the Second New Deal legislation relied more heavily on the Keynesian style of deficit spending than the First New Deal did. Roosevelt altered his policy making in part because of complaints from critics and in part because, by 1935, it was clear that more Americans still needed federal relief assistance. Roosevelt thus aimed approximately half the Second New Deal programs and policies at long-term reform.

NEW DEAL CRITICS

Predictably, Roosevelt's New Deal came under attack from the right, from Republicans, conservative Democrats, bankers, and Wall Street financiers who claimed that it doled out too many federal handouts. Many of these critics also feared that the policy and programs involved were a dangerous step toward **socialism** and the destruction of the American capitalist system. Such misgivings were understandable given the political atmosphere in the 1930s, as communism was becoming a more imminent threat. In fact, Soviet agents in the United States went so far as to launch a "popular front" campaign to actively support the president. Moreover, an unprecedented number of people joined the **American Communist Party** during the decade.

Perhaps more surprising, the New Deal also came under attack from the far left. Many socialist activists denounced the New Deal because they believed that it was too conservative and that it did not provide *enough* relief and assistance. Over the years, many historians have tended to agree with this argument. Several have argued that the Great Depression would not have been so devastating for so long had Roosevelt handed more federal money out to a greater number of Americans.

COUGHLIN AND LONG

One of the most vocal of Roosevelt's critics was Father **Charles Coughlin**. A Catholic priest from Michigan, Coughlin began broadcasting a weekly radio show in 1930 that outwardly criticized the New Deal. Within a few short years, Coughlin had amassed a following of 40 million listeners who agreed with his anti–New Deal opinions. He blamed the Great Depression on Wall Street, crooked financiers, and Jews and campaigned for the nationalization of the entire American banking system.

Senator **Huey P. Long** of Louisiana was another major thorn in Roosevelt's side, albeit from the left rather than the right. Long was among those who believed that the New Deal was not doing enough to help Americans. Believing that income inequality had caused the depression, he promoted his own **"Share the Wealth" program** (sometimes referred to as the **"Every Man a King" program**), which would levy enormous taxes on the rich so that every American family could earn at least $5,000 a year. Long enjoyed enormous popularity during the first few years of Roosevelt's first term but was assassinated in 1935.

THE WORKS PROGRESS ADMINISTRATION

The first major legislation that Roosevelt and Congress passed in the Second New Deal—in response to the critics—was the **Works Progress Administration (WPA)**. Created in 1935, the WPA was an effort to appease the **"Longites"** who clamored for more direct assistance from the federal government. The WPA was similar to the Public Works Administration of the First New Deal, this time hiring nearly 10 million Americans to construct new public buildings, roads, and bridges. Congress dumped over $10 billion into the projects in just under a decade.

THE SOCIAL SECURITY ACT

Congress also passed the **Social Security Act** in 1935, creating a federal retiree pension system for many workers, funded by a double tax on every working American's paycheck. The act also created an unemployment insurance plan to provide temporary assistance to those who were out of work, while also making funds available to the blind and physically disabled. Furthermore, Congress agreed to match federal dollars for every state dollar allocated to workers' compensation funds.

Despite its vocal critics, the Social Security Act had an enormous impact on Great Depression–era Americans and future generations. It brought the most sweeping change of the Second New Deal legislation as it not only gave income to some of the most destitute in society but also forever changed the way Americans thought about work and retirement. The paycheck taxes were advertised as a personal retirement savings plan even though those tax dollars were actually being redistributed as soon as they were collected. Nevertheless, retirement came to be seen as something every worker could enjoy. Still, many criticized the Social Security system for not extending pensions to enough people, particularly unskilled black and women laborers.

LEGISLATION FOR FARMERS AND HOMEOWNERS

The Second New Deal provided even more assistance to farmers. After the Supreme Court declared the Agricultural Adjustment Administration unconstitutional in 1936, Democrats immediately responded with the passage of the **Soil Conservation and Domestic Allotment Act** that same year. This act continued to subsidize farmers to curb overproduction and also paid them either to plant soil-enriching crops (instead of wheat) or to not grow any crops at all. In 1938, Congress also created a **Second Agricultural Adjustment Administration** to reduce crop acreage. Meanwhile, the **United States Housing Authority (USHA)**, created by Congress in 1937, gave assistance to American urbanites, building new houses for over half a million Americans.

THE INDIAN REORGANIZATION ACT

Native Americans also received federal assistance during Roosevelt's second term. In 1934, Congress passed the **Indian Reorganization**

Act (IRA) to promote tribal organization and give federal recognition to tribal governments. The IRA also reversed the 1887 Dawes Severalty Act, changing the relationship between various tribes and the federal government. The Dawes Act had weakened tribal affiliations because it stated that only individual Native Americans—not tribal councils—could own land.

Despite Roosevelt's efforts to alleviate Native American suffering, however, the IRA was only partially successful. Some tribes had difficulty understanding the terms of the new treaty, while others, such as the Navajo in the Southwest, flat-out rejected it. Many tribes saw more immediate benefit from relief programs such as the Civilian Conservation Corps, Public Works Administration, and Works Progress Administration, in which nearly 100,000 young Native American men participated.

LABOR REFORMS

These labor reforms had a lasting effect on America. The Wagner Act paved the way for more effective collective bargaining and striking, and within a year, fledgling labor unions had I-line workers in the General Motors automobile factory, for example, used the Wagner Act to initiate a series of sit-down strikes, in which workers would sit at their stations and refuse to leave, preventing the company from hiring new, non-union "scab" workers to fill in for the strikers. By 1937, General Motors had recognized its workers' right to organize.

THE ELECTION OF 1936

With the 1936 presidential election on the horizon, Republicans stood virtually no chance against Roosevelt and his party. Democrats' efforts to provide relief, recovery, and reform were highly visible. Roosevelt had especially strong support among blacks (voting as Democrats in large numbers for the first time), unskilled laborers, and residents of the West and South. The Republican nominee was Kansas governor **Alfred M. Landon**, a moderate who campaigned on an anti–New Deal platform. Not surprisingly, Roosevelt won a landslide victory, with 523 electoral votes to Landon's 8. Roosevelt's resounding victory proved that Americans widely supported the New Deal.

SUMMARY & ANALYSIS

THE DEMISE OF THE NEW DEAL: 1935–1939

EVENTS

1936	*Butler v. United States* ruling
1937	Roosevelt initiates court-packing scheme Roosevelt Recession begins
1939	Congress passes the Hatch Act

KEY PEOPLE

Franklin Delano Roosevelt 32nd U.S. president; attempted to fill Supreme Court with like-minded justices to ensure longevity of New Deal policies; brought on brief economic recession

A WEAKENED NEW DEAL

By 1935, New Deal critics were becoming more numerous and vocal. Congressmen, including even some Democrats, had overcome the initial panic and were becoming more fiscally conservative as **Franklin Delano Roosevelt**'s deficit spending soared. More important, aging, conservative appointees dominated the Supreme Court and had begun to strike down several key laws of the **First New Deal**.

In the 1935 ***Schechter v. United States*** ruling, for example, a majority of justices declared that the National Recovery Act was unconstitutional. They argued that the act gave too much power to the president and was an attempt to control intrastate commerce. The following year, justices also struck down the Agricultural Adjustment Administration in ***Butler v. United States*** on the grounds that it was unconstitutional and tried to exert federal control of agricultural production.

ROOSEVELT'S COURT-PACKING SCHEME

Roosevelt believed that the National Recovery Act and the Agricultural Adjustment Administration were crucial to reviving the American economy and feared that any more conservative Supreme Court rulings would cripple or even kill New Deal policy entirely. In 1937, to prevent this from happening, the president petitioned Congress to alter the makeup of the Supreme Court on the pretense that the justices, old age was affecting their ability to work and concentrate. Roosevelt asked for the power to appoint as many as **six new justices**, bringing the total to fifteen, and to replace justices over the age of seventy. The true aim of the request was obvious: it would enable Roosevelt to effectively stack the deck to ensure that only pro–New Dealers would sit on the Court.

The **court-packing scheme** backfired. Rather than win over Democrats and New Dealers in Congress, Roosevelt shocked supporters with his attempt at misusing his executive powers. The president's blatant disregard for the cherished separation of powers stunned even the American people. Roosevelt repeatedly denied charges that he was trying to bend the entire federal government to his will and defended his belief that aging justices were often incapable of performing their duties. The court-packing debate dragged on for several months before Congress and Roosevelt reached a compromise. Congress made minor reforms in the lower courts but left the Supreme Court untouched.

CONSEQUENCES OF THE COURT-PACKING SCHEME

The court-packing scheme took a severe toll on Roosevelt's popularity and marked the beginning of the end of the New Deal. Politicians and regular Americans alike were keenly aware that the federal government under the tight control of a single individual would be nothing more than a dictatorship, no matter how benevolent or well intentioned the leader happened to be. Roosevelt's clumsy attempts to disguise his intentions had the effect only of making him look guilty. As the public grew suspicious of "dictator" Roosevelt, fellow Democrats in Congress began to vote more conservatively, and the chances of any more significant New Deal legislation being passed became slim.

Ironically, the court-packing scheme may have helped Roosevelt in one way. Supreme Court Justice **Owen Roberts**, who had notoriously struck down New Deal laws in the past, mysteriously began to vote in favor of the Wagner Act and the Social Security Act after Roosevelt announced his plan to replace six justices. Historians are still uncertain as to why Roberts suddenly looked favorably upon the New Deal, but few believe it was mere coincidence.

THE ROOSEVELT RECESSION

In 1937, Roosevelt began to scale back **deficit spending**, because he believed that the worst of the Great Depression had passed and because he was receiving pressure from conservatives in Congress (and even from ardent New Dealers in his own cabinet). The size of the **Works Progress Administration**, for example, was severely reduced, as were agricultural subsidies.

This decision to cut back spending turned out to be premature, however, as the economy buckled again, resulting in what became known as the **Roosevelt Recession**. The stock market crashed for a second time in 1937, and the price of consumer goods dropped significantly. Contrary to conservative beliefs, the economy simply had not pulled far enough out of the depression to survive on its own. The embattled Roosevelt only made himself look worse by trying to place the blame on spendthrift business leaders. The American people were not convinced, and as a result, Democrats lost a significant number of seats in the House and Senate in the 1938 congressional elections. This return of Republican power effectively killed the New Deal.

The Hatch Act

Republicans in Congress further weakened Roosevelt's executive powers with the **Hatch Act** of 1939. The act forbade most civil servants from participating in political campaigns and public office holders (i.e., Roosevelt and New Dealers) from using federal dollars to fund their reelection campaigns. The bill also made it illegal for Americans who received federal assistance to donate money to politicians. Conservatives hoped that these measures would divorce the functions of government from the campaign frenzy and ultimately dislodge entrenched New Dealers who preyed on a desperate public for votes.

No End to the Depression

Despite the numerous positive effects that the New Deal had, it failed to end the Great Depression. Millions of Americans were still hungry, homeless, and without jobs as late as December 1941, when the United States entered World War II. Many historians and economists have suggested that the New Deal would have been more successful if Roosevelt had put a greater amount of money into the economy, but this conclusion is debatable. Only after the surge in demand for war-related goods such as munitions, ships, tanks, and airplanes did the economy finally right itself and begin to grow.

The Legacy of the New Deal

The New Deal was a crucial turning point in the history of the U.S. government. Politics had never before been so involved in—or exerted more control over—the daily lives of regular Americans as it was during Roosevelt's terms in office in the 1930s. Critics lamented that the United States had transformed itself into a welfare state. Indeed, the budget deficit increased dramatically every year, and the national debt more than doubled in just ten years.

However, the New Deal did in fact help millions of Americans survive the Great Depression. Unlike his predecessor, Herbert Hoover, Roosevelt tried to directly help as many people as the conservatives in Congress and the Supreme Court would allow him to. His New Deal legislation helped create new jobs, build houses and shelters for the homeless, and distribute food to the hungry. New Deal policy also raised agricultural commodity prices, put banks back on solid footing, and greatly improved the national infrastructure. Moreover, the New Deal created a number of long-standing government institutions, such as Social Security, that we still have today.

STUDY QUESTIONS & ESSAY TOPICS

Always use specific historical examples to support your arguments.

STUDY QUESTIONS

1. *In your opinion, was Roosevelt's New Deal a success or a failure?*

Although Franklin Roosevelt's New Deal provided relief to millions of Americans, the New Deal ultimately failed because it did not end the Great Depression. The New Deal was simply not enough to cure the economy of its maladies.

Admittedly, the New Deal was highly successful in achieving the limited goal of providing immediate relief to millions of hungry, homeless, and jobless Americans. The Federal Emergency Relief Act, for example, earmarked about half a billion dollars to distribute to states on the verge of bankruptcy and directly to Americans who needed government handouts the most. The Public Works Administration, Works Progress Administration, Civilian Conservation Corps, and Civil Works Administration also provided invaluable employment to millions of young men during the depression. Most of Roosevelt's new alphabet agencies, however, were just quick fixes to remedy the most visible effects of the Great Depression without doing anything to solve the problems that had caused the economic collapse in the first place.

Roosevelt and New Dealers did make attempts to put the nation back on track toward long-term recovery and to reform the American financial system. Along with Congress, Roosevelt created the Federal Deposit Insurance Corporation (passed under the Glass-Steagall Banking Reform Act) to prevent future bank failures and the Securities and Exchange Commission to regulate commodity trading on the stock market. The Wagner Act and Fair Labor Standard Acts, meanwhile, protected the rights of laborers, and the Social Security Act set up retirement pensions for the elderly and disabled.

These reforms were still not enough, however, as the Roosevelt Recession of 1937 demonstrated. Believing the worst of the depression to be over and wanting to appease critics, Roosevelt cut back deficit spending in the hopes that the government had already injected enough dollars into the economy for it to right itself. This hope proved mistaken, as the stock market collapsed again and millions of people lost their jobs. Perhaps contemporary critics such as Huey P. Long were correct: more federal dollars were needed to prime the economic pump. As it turns out, however, only the wartime demands placed on manufacturing and labor during World War II pulled the American economy out of its hole.

2.   *Why did the New Deal lose steam in 1938 and 1939?*

The New Deal faded away in the late 1930s primarily because Roosevelt grew overconfident in his own abilities to end the Great Depression. As a result, he made several bad decisions that turned a significant group of Americans against him and the New Deal.

When Roosevelt was first elected president in 1933, most Americans believed he was the only person who could save the economy. As governor of New York, he had successfully used Keynesian-style deficit spending to inject money into the economy and reduce the devastating impacts of the depression. He had also had some success initiating across-the-board reforms to make sure the state would never again be hit hard by a financial crisis like the Crash of 1929. Compared to the conservative Herbert Hoover, who refused to provide any direct assistance at all, Roosevelt seemed like a godsend.

Roosevelt delivered on his promises in many ways and thus earned the solid support of the American people. During his First Hundred Days in office, he put the nation's banks back on solid footing and created a variety of new alphabet agencies such as the Civilian Conservation Corps, Public Works Administration, and Federal Emergency Relief Administration to dole out jobs and money. He also reformed Wall Street and propped up American agriculture. His Second New Deal initiatives were also so popular that he received all but eight electoral votes in the presidential election of 1936.

During his second term, however, Roosevelt overstepped his bounds and took controversial actions that proved very unpopular. With Congress under his control, he had only to defeat the conservative Supreme Court in order to ensure that his New Deal policies would endure. With this in mind, in early 1937 he requested Congress to grant him the power to add as many as six pro–New Deal justices to the Supreme Court and to force all justices over the age of seventy to retire. This action shocked Congress, which flatly denied the request. Even fellow Democrats were astonished by Roosevelt's flagrant attempt to undermine the system of checks and balances and separation of powers. The American public was also horrified, especially as Roosevelt repeatedly denied his obvious intentions for wanting to pack the Court with New Deal supporters.

This move cost Roosevelt dearly: he lost many supporters, not only among the American people but also among congressmen in his own party, on whom he relied to pass his legislation. Soon thereafter, Roosevelt made an additional mistake in reducing the amount of federal dollars he pumped into the economy in the hopes that the economy could finally pull out of the depression by itself. Lacking enough support, the economy crumpled again, causing the Roosevelt Recession. The president's attempt to point fingers only frustrated Americans more. As a result, voters ousted many Democrats from Congress in the midterm elections of 1938, effectively ending any chance of passing additional New Deal legislation. Had Roosevelt not overstepped his bounds via the court-packing scheme nor vehemently denied responsibility for the 1937 recession, the New Deal might have survived longer than it did.

3. *Which had greater immediate effect on the American economy, the First New Deal or the Second New Deal? Which had greater long-term significance after the end of the Great Depression?*

Even though the First New Deal (1933–1934) and the Second New Deal (1935–1938) were both part of Roosevelt's plan to reinvigorate the economy with Keynesian-style federal deficit spending, the two bundles of legislation were in many ways quite different. First New Deal legislation, for example, was passed primarily in order to provide immediate relief to the bankrupt states and directly to the people. On the other hand, much of the Second New Deal legislation was meant to reform the economy and prevent future depressions. As a result, the First New Deal had the more immediate effect on the U.S. economy, but the Second New Deal had much greater significance after the Great Depression.

QUESTIONS & ESSAYS

Most legislation passed during Roosevelt's First Hundred Days was intended to help the poorest Americans, to whom Herbert Hoover had refused to give assistance. The Federal Emergency Relief Administration, for example, distributed over half a billion dollars in grants (rather than loans) to the individual state governments and directly to the people. The Civilian Conservation Corps, Civil Works Administration, and Public Works Administration were also established to give jobs to the unemployed and improve the national infrastructure. The first Agricultural Adjustment Administration provided subsidies to farmers to cut crop production and artificially raise the price of agricultural goods. These programs had an enormous impact on those Americans who needed immediate relief the most. On the other hand, benefits from these "alphabet agencies" were all short-term benefits. The agencies distributed money to those who needed it but made no attempt to cure the depression at the source.

Much of the legislation passed in the Second New Deal, however, did try to reform the system to prevent another catastrophic depression from occurring in the future. The Wagner Act and Fair Labor Standards Act altered the power imbalance between big business and labor by recognizing workers' right to bargain collectively and by establishing a minimum wage and forty-hour workweek in select industries. These new laws gave a boost to blossoming labor organizations such as the Congress of Industrial Organizations, which has since become one of the largest unions in the United States. The Social Security Act of 1935 was even more sweeping, as it created a federal pension system funded by employers and taxpayers to keep the disabled and retired workers from becoming destitute.

Not all Second New Deal legislation focused on reform, however. In fact, Roosevelt and Congress created several new relief organizations, such as the Works Progress Administration and the United States Housing Authority, in response to criticism that the First New Deal had not helped Americans enough. Likewise, some reform-oriented agencies had been created in the First New Deal in 1933 and 1934, such as the Federal Deposit Insurance Corporation, Tennessee Valley Authority, and Securities and Exchange Commission. For the most part, however, Roosevelt and fellow Democrats legislated the First New Deal to provide immediate relief and the Second New Deal to initiate long-term reform.

QUESTIONS & ESSAYS

SUGGESTED ESSAY TOPICS

1. *Explain how three of the following affected American politics or society during the 1920s:*

   Warren G. Harding
   the Teapot Dome scandal
   the Five-Power Naval Treaty
   the Sacco-Vanzetti Trial
   Prohibition
   the Scopes Monkey Trial

2. *What were some of the causes of the Great Depression? How did Hoover's policies worsen the effects?*

3. *How did the Great Depression and New Deal transform American politics?*

4. *Some contemporary critics accused Roosevelt of being a dictator. Defend or refute this claim.*

REVIEW & RESOURCES

QUIZ

1. All of the following were causes of the Great Depression *except*

   A. Poor banking practices
   B. Depressed precious metal prices
   C. European countries' inability to pay their debts
   D. Overproduction in factories and on farms

2. The "Bonus Army" marched on Washington, D.C., to pressure Congress to

   A. Pay World War I veterans their army pensions early
   B. Pass the Norris–La Guardia Anti-Injunction Act to protect organized labor
   C. Dole out federal aid to the homeless and depressed living in "Hoovervilles"
   D. Help destitute farmers survive in the Dust Bowl region

3. How did Herbert Hoover believe that the economy could be revived?

   A. Through government intervention to directly assist the poor
   B. By supporting industry in the hopes that federal dollars at the top would "trickle down" to the poorest Americans
   C. By forcing Britain and France to repay their war debts
   D. By shifting the base of the economy away from heavy industry toward the production of consumer goods

4. Why did topsoil turn to a fine layer of infertile dust in the Dust Bowl region of the United States?

   A. Tornadoes had ravaged the region
   B. The area was poorly irrigated
   C. Farmers had not planted soil-replenishing crops
   D. All of the above

5. Franklin Delano Roosevelt won a landslide victory in 1932 because Americans

    A.   Were dissatisfied with Hoover's "ride-it-out" policy
    B.   Distrusted Hoover after the "Battle of Anacostia Flats"
    C.   Wanted more direct federal assistance
    D.   All of the above

6. The Ku Klux Klan of the 1920s was *not* different from the Klan of the nineteenth century in that

    A.   The KKK of the 1920s was also anti-Jewish
    B.   The KKK of the 1920s was also anti-black
    C.   The KKK of the 1920s was also anti-immigration
    D.   All of the above

7. What prompted the 1919–1920 Red Scare in the United States?

    A.   Eugene V. Debs and the rise of the Socialist Party
    B.   The 1917 Bolshevik Revolution in Russia
    C.   The influx of southern and eastern European immigrants to the United States
    D.   All of the above

8. The Eighteenth Amendment

    A.   Gave women the right to vote
    B.   Allowed Americans to elect U.S. senators directly
    C.   Prohibited the manufacture, sale, and consumption of alcohol
    D.   Ended Prohibition

9. In which U.S. election were women first allowed to vote?

    A.   1920
    B.   1924
    C.   1928
    D.   1932

10. The Emergency Quota Act severely reduced immigration from

   A. Northern Europe
   B. Southern and eastern Europe
   C. Ireland and Germany
   D. Latin America

11. What did the Immigration Act of 1924 do?

   A. Increased national immigration quotas from their 1921 levels
   B. Decreased national immigration quotas from their 1921 levels
   C. Forbade Latin Americans from entering the United States
   D. Forbade Chinese immigrants from entering the United States

12. The Scopes Monkey Trial illustrated the heated debate between

   A. Christian fundamentalists and those who believed in natural selection
   B. Democrats and Republicans regarding immigration
   C. The wets and the drys regarding Prohibition
   D. Liberals and conservatives regarding the New Deal

13. What caused the so-called Roosevelt Recession of 1937?

   A. Overspeculation in western lands
   B. Germany's inability to repay war reparations to Britain and France
   C. Overspending
   D. The U.S. government's overly hasty retreat from deficit spending

REVIEW & RESOURCES

14. What did the 1939 Hatch Act do?

    A. Reduced the exorbitantly high tax on foreign goods under the Smoot-Hawley Tariff

    B. Further reduced immigration

    C. Barred federal officials from participating in political campaigns

    D. Helped farmers by paying them to burn surplus crops

15. The Five-Power Naval Treaty of 1922 reflected

    A. America's unwillingness to remain overinvolved in international affairs

    B. Harding's interest in protecting American territorial possessions in the Pacific

    C. Japan's willingness to scale down military operations in Asia

    D. Europe's willingness to uphold the Open Door policy in China

16. The Dawes Plan

    A. Outlawed tribal ownership of Native American lands

    B. Revitalized the financial sector of the American economy in 1933–1934

    C. Outlined Roosevelt's three-step program to provide relief, recovery, and reform to end the depression

    D. Rescheduled Germany's war reparation payments to Britain and France

17. Henry Ford changed industrial America by perfecting a method of

    A. Building machines with interchangeable parts

    B. Vertical integration

    C. Horizontal integration

    D. Assembly-line production

18. Why did more and more Americans move out of the cities and into the suburbs in the 1920s?

    A.   Cars allowed them to commute

    B.   Costs of living in the city soared to unprecedented heights

    C.   Cities grew increasingly dangerous due to the rise of organized crime

    D.   Americans feared the influx of southern and eastern European immigrants

19. Warren G. Harding's administration and personal reputation were tainted by

    A.   The convictions of Sacco and Vanzetti

    B.   The Scopes Monkey Trial

    C.   The Teapot Dome scandal

    D.   The Crash of 1929

20. The Twenty-First Amendment

    A.   Gave women the right to vote

    B.   Allowed Americans to elect U.S. senators directly

    C.   Prohibited the manufacture, sale, and consumption of alcohol

    D.   Ended Prohibition

21. What did the Fordney-McCumber Tariff do?

    A.   Sparked a tariff war between the United States and Western Europe

    B.   Drove the tariff rate up to nearly 40 percent

    C.   Stifled the European economy

    D.   All of the above

22. The tax on foreign goods under the Smoot-Hawley Tariff of 1930

    A. Was higher than it was under the Fordney-McCumber Tariff of 1922

    B. Was lower than it was under the Fordney-McCumber Tariff

    C. Was the same as the Fordney-McCumber Tariff

    D. Sparked the Great Depression

23. Attacks from critics such as Huey P. Long and Father Charles Coughlin were partly responsible for

    A. The Civilian Conservation Corps

    B. The Second New Deal

    C. Prohibition

    D. The Good Neighbor Policy

24. To which act was the Wagner Act most similar?

    A. The Hatch Act

    B. The Fair Labor Standards Act

    C. The Norris–La Guardia Anti-Injunction Act

    D. The Esch-Cummins Transportation Act

25. One unintended consequence of Prohibition was

    A. A rise in organized crime

    B. Class riots in New York and Chicago

    C. A rise in the sale and consumption of tobacco

    D. Republican losses in the congressional elections of 1926

26. What did Hoover's Reconstruction Finance Corporation do?

    A. Distributed government funds directly to the poorest Americans during the depression

    B. Paid farmers to burn surplus crops to raise agricultural commodity prices

    C. Loaned money to corporations, banks, and the states

    D. Distributed money to victims of the Dust Bowl

27. The Indian Reorganization Act of 1934 replaced

    A. The Dawes Plan
    B. The Dawes Severalty Act
    C. The Hatch Act
    D. The Norris–La Guardia Anti-Injunction Act

28. The election of 1936

    A. Returned the White House to Republicans
    B. Demonstrated that Americans' support for Roosevelt was waning
    C. Had one of the lowest voter turnouts in history
    D. Proved that Americans wholeheartedly supported the New Deal

29. What did the Fair Labor Standards Act do?

    A. Outlawed workers' right to strike
    B. Established the forty-hour workweek and a minimum wage
    C. Created the Congress of Industrial Workers
    D. Upheld workers' right to strike

30. The Soil Conservation and Domestic Allotment Act subsidized farmers to

    A. Grow only wheat and corn in order to curb nationwide hunger
    B. Grow cotton to sell in Europe
    C. Plant soil-replenishing crops such as soybeans
    D. All of the above

31. Economist John Maynard Keynes believed that depressed economies could be jump-started by

    A. Deficit spending
    B. Printing more paper money
    C. Taking the nation off the gold standard
    D. Protecting organized labor

REVIEW & RESOURCES

32. Most New Deal legislation in the First Hundred Days was passed to

   A. Provide immediate relief
   B. Put the economy on the road to long-term recovery
   C. Initiate reforms to prevent another depression
   D. All of the above

33. Hoover's attempts to end the depression differed from Roosevelt's methods in that

   A. Hoover pumped money into the economy by creating new jobs and welfare programs, whereas Roosevelt merely tried to prop up failing corporations and banks
   B. Roosevelt pumped money into the economy by creating new jobs and welfare programs, whereas Hoover merely tried to prop up failing corporations and banks
   C. Hoover tried to help farmers first, whereas Roosevelt wanted to help factory workers first
   D. Hoover thought the federal government should assume control of all banks in the country, whereas Roosevelt believed that richer Americans should pay heavier taxes in order to redistribute wealth more evenly

34. How did the New Deal assist farmers?

   A. By subsidizing them to cut back production
   B. By subsiding them to plant soil-enriching crops
   C. By artificially inflating agricultural prices
   D. All of the above

35. All of the following were consequences of the Tennessee Valley Authority *except*

   A. It spawned a flurry of dam-building throughout the West
   B. It brought electricity and modernization to one of the nation's poorest regions
   C. It convinced Republicans that deficit spending on social welfare programs could have huge benefits
   D. It provided almost full employment in the Tennessee River valley

36. Congress passed or created all of the following in 1933 as part of the First New Deal *except*

    A. The Public Works Administration (PWA)
    B. The Social Security Act
    C. The Federal Emergency Relief Act (FERA)
    D. The Civilian Conservation Corp (CCC)

37. The CCC, the PWA, the CWA, and the WPA all were similar in that they all were

    A. Created to reform the financial sector of the economy to prevent another depression
    B. Created under the First New Deal
    C. Created to provide immediate economic relief
    D. Shot down by the Supreme Court only a few years after their creation

38. Roosevelt reformed the banking and financial sectors of the economy in all of the following ways *except*

    A. Providing insurance for all savings account deposits up to $5,000
    B. Putting the United States on the silver standard
    C. Taking the United States off the gold standard
    D. Regulating and supervising stock market transactions

39. Why did many Americans criticize the Agricultural Adjustment Administration?

    A. Because many of the neediest sharecroppers and tenant farmers received no benefits
    B. Because the AAA subsidized farmers to cut production by destroying excess crops while millions of people didn't have enough food
    C. Because the AAA established artificially high prices
    D. All of the above

40. Buying stocks "on margin" refers to the practice of

    A. Purchasing stocks without researching companies or market trends beforehand

    B. Taking out bank loans to buy stocks

    C. Taking out illegal loans from gangsters in order to buy stocks

    D. Using the prospect of future stock earnings to buy more stocks

41. What did the Glass-Steagall Act do?

    A. Outlawed the practice of buying stocks on margin

    B. Established the FDIC to insure personal savings accounts

    C. Protected workers' rights to strike and bargain collectively

    D. Created the Public Works Administration

42. The Sacco-Vanzetti trial demonstrated

    A. Americans' prejudice against immigrants

    B. The revamped KKK's cruelty toward Italian Catholics

    C. The rise of organized crime

    D. The heated debate between Christian fundamentalists and those who believed in Darwin's theory of natural selection

43. All of the following contributed to the demise of the New Deal *except*

    A. The Roosevelt Recession

    B. Roosevelt's court-packing scheme

    C. The Wagner Act

    D. *Schechter v. United States*

44. What did Roosevelt's "fireside chats" do?

    A. Restored confidence in the banking system

    B. Demonstrated the new power of radio

    C. Boosted American's confidence in the president

    D. All of the above

45. All of the following were components of the Second New Deal *except*

    A. The Wagner Act
    B. The Social Security Act
    C. The Hatch Act
    D. The Soil Conservation and Domestic Allotment Act

46. The so-called Lost Generation authors of the 1920s

    A. Described utopian societies of the future
    B. Were disillusioned with America after World War I
    C. Railed against social injustices
    D. Predicted the Great Depression

47. Americans' antiwar sentiments in the 1920s were reflected in

    A. The Nine-Power Naval Treaty
    B. The Twenty-First Amendment
    C. The Good Neighbor Policy
    D. The Kellogg-Briand Pact

48. What was an effect of the Roosevelt Recession?

    A. It helped Republicans return to power in Congress
    B. It encouraged Democrats to legislate the Second New Deal
    C. It convinced Roosevelt that Keynesian-style deficit spending was failing
    D. It prompted the Red Scare

49. In the Four-Power Treaty of 1922, France, Britain, and the United States agreed

    A. To reduce their number of battleships in the Pacific
    B. To carve China into separate spheres of influence
    C. Not to fortify their territorial possessions in the Pacific even though Japan could
    D. To prepare for a possible war with Japan over Southeast Asia

50. Franklin Delano Roosevelt was related to previous president

    A. William McKinley
    B. Benjamin Harrison
    C. Eleanor Roosevelt
    D. Theodore Roosevelt

ANSWER KEY

1. B; 2. A; 3. B; 4. C; 5. D; 6. D; 7. B; 8. C; 9. A; 10. B; 11. B; 12. A; 13. D;
14. C; 15. A; 16. D; 17. D; 18. A; 19. C; 20. D; 21. D; 22. A; 23. B; 24. C;
25. A; 26. C; 27. B; 28. D; 29. B; 30. C; 31. A; 32. A; 33. B; 34. D; 35. C;
36. B; 37. C; 38. B; 39. D; 40. D; 41. B; 42. A; 43. C; 44. D; 45. C; 46. B;
47. D; 48. A; 49. C; 50. D

Suggestions for Further Reading

GALBRAITH, JOHN KENNETH. *The Great Crash: 1929*. Boston: Mariner Books, 1997.

KENNEDY, DAVID M. *Freedom from Fear: The American People in Depression and War, 1929–1945*. New York: Oxford University Press, 2001.

KINDLEBERGER, CHARLES P. *The World in Depression, 1929–1939*. Berkeley: University of California Press, 1986.

LEUCHTENBURG, WILLIAM E. *Franklin D. Roosevelt and the New Deal*. New York: Perennial, 1963.

SCHLESINGER, ARTHUR M., JR. *The Age of Roosevelt, Volume I: The Crisis of the Old Order, 1919–1933*. Boston: Mariner Books, 2003.

———. *The Age of Roosevelt, Volume II: The Coming of the New Deal, 1933–1935*. Boston: Mariner Books, 2003.

———. *The Age of Roosevelt, Volume III: The Politics of Upheaval, 1935–1936*. Boston: Mariner Books, 2003.

WORSTER, DONALD. *Dust Bowl: The Southern Plains in the 1930s*. New York: Oxford University Press, 1982.

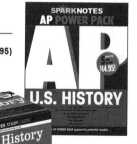